ENVIRONMENTAL FOOTPRINTS

How Big Is Your Food Footprint?

Paul Mason

Marshall Cavendish
Benchmark

New York

This edition first published in 2010 in the United States of America by Marshall Cavendish Benchmark.

Marshall Cavendish Benchmark
99 White Plains Road
Tarrytown, NY 10591
www.marshallcavendish.us

First published in 2008 by
MACMILLAN EDUCATION AUSTRALIA PTY LTD
15–19 Claremont Street, South Yarra 3141

Visit our website at www.macmillan.com.au or go directly to www.macmillanlibrary.com.au

Associated companies and representatives throughout the world.

Copyright © Paul Mason 2008

Library of Congress Cataloging-in-Publication Data

Mason, Paul.
  How big is your food footprint? / by Paul Mason.
  p. cm. – (Environmental footprints)
  Includes index.
  ISBN 978-0-7614-4413-8
  1. Food industry and trade–Environmental aspects–Juvenile literature. 2. Sustainable agriculture–Juvenile literature. 3. Food industry and trade–Environmental aspects–Case studies–Juvenile literature. 4. Sustainable agriculture–Case studies–Juvenile literature. I. Title.
  TD195.F57M37 2009
  664.0028'6–dc22
                                                    2008048103

Edited by Anna Fern
Text and cover design by Cristina Neri, Canary Graphic Design
Page layout by Domenic Lauricella
Photo research by Legend Images
Illustrations by Nives Porcellato and Andrew Craig

Printed in the United States

Acknowledgments
The author and the publisher are grateful to the following for permission to reproduce copyright material:

Front cover photograph: Earth from space © Jan Rysavy/iStockphoto; colored footprint © Rich Harris/iStockphoto. Images repeated throughout title.

Photos courtesy of:
© Mike Langford/Auscape, **11**; © Rssfhs/Dreamstime.com, **22**; Tim Graham/Getty Images, **15**; David Silverman/Getty Images, **7**; Dod Miller/Reportage/Getty Images, **8**; © Brasil2/iStockphoto, **10**; © calvio/iStockphoto, **5**; © Sean Locke/iStockphoto, **28**; © Willi Schmitz/iStockphoto, **12**; © Subic/iStockphoto, **18**; Patagonia, **27**; Rob Cruse Photography, **17**, **26**; © Hannamariah/Shutterstock, **20**; © Tischenko Irina/Shutterstock, **3** (top right), **16**; © jbor/Shutterstock, **30**; © Semen Lixodeev/Shutterstock, **25**; © Ismael Montero Verdu/Shutterstock, **24**; © Martine Oger/Shutterstock, **19**; © PhotoCreate/Shutterstock, **23**; © Vova Pomortzeff/Shutterstock, **13**; © Radu Razvan/Shutterstock, **6**; © Leah-Anne Thompson/Shutterstock, **29**; USDA, photo by Ken Hammond, **14**.

Please note
At the time of printing, the Internet addresses appearing in this book were correct. Owing to the dynamic nature of the Internet, however, we cannot guarantee that all these addresses will remain correct.

1 3 5 6 4 2

Contents

Environmental Footprints   4

The Food Industry   6

Farming   10

Case Study Farming in a Dry Land   11

Case Study An Organic Farm   15

Food Processing   16

Food Transportation   20

Case Study Farmers' Markets   23

Food Packaging   24

Case Study Clothes from Plastic Drink Bottles   27

How Big Is Your Food Footprint?   28

Future Food Footprints   30

Glossary   31

Index   32

Glossary Words
When a word is printed in **bold**, you can look up its meaning in the Glossary on page 31.

Environmental Footprints

This book is about the footprints people leave behind them. But these are special footprints. They are the footprints people leave on the **environment**.

Heavy Footprints

Some people leave heavy, long-lasting footprints. They do this by:

⊕ acting in ways that harm the environment

⊕ using up lots of **natural resources**, including water, land, and energy

It can be hundreds of years before the environment recovers from heavy footprints.

Light Footprints

Other people leave light, short-lived footprints. They do this by:

⊕ behaving in ways that harm the environment as little as possible

⊕ using the smallest amount of natural resources they can

The environment recovers from light footprints much more quickly.

As the world's population grows, more natural resources will be needed. It will be important not to waste resources if we are to leave light footprints.

The world's population is expected to continue growing in the future.

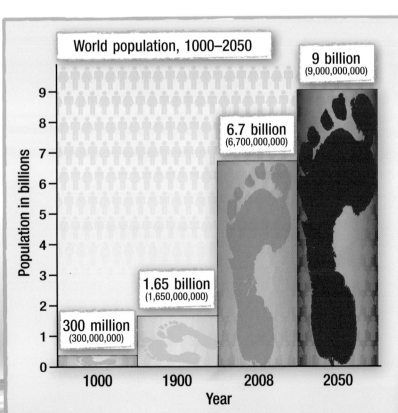

World population, 1000–2050

9 billion
(9,000,000,000)

6.7 billion
(6,700,000,000)

1.65 billion
(1,650,000,000)

300 million
(300,000,000)

Population in billions

1000   1900   2008   2050
Year

The choices people make about what they eat can have a big effect on their food footprint.

What Makes Up a Food Footprint?

A food footprint is made up of the effects of the food people eat on the environment. It includes every step from farm to table, such as:

⊕ the way the food is grown

⊕ how the food is transported

⊕ how the food is prepared for sale, including how it is wrapped

⊕ the way the food is cooked

All these things have an effect on the environment.
The bigger the effect, the heavier the footprint left behind.

What sort of food footsteps are you taking? Read on to find out!

The Food Industry

The food industry is made up of everything needed for food to be grown and sold. It includes farming, transportation, **processing**, **packaging**, and selling the food in stores.

The Food Industry Today

Today, science and technology have made the food industry a giant international business. A visitor from one hundred years ago would be amazed by the changes in how food is produced and supplied.

Farming

Farmers today grow more food on their land than ever before, using chemical **fertilizers** and **irrigation**. Chemical **pesticides** stop insects and other pests from damaging or destroying the crops. Machines help farmers to **harvest** their crops more easily.

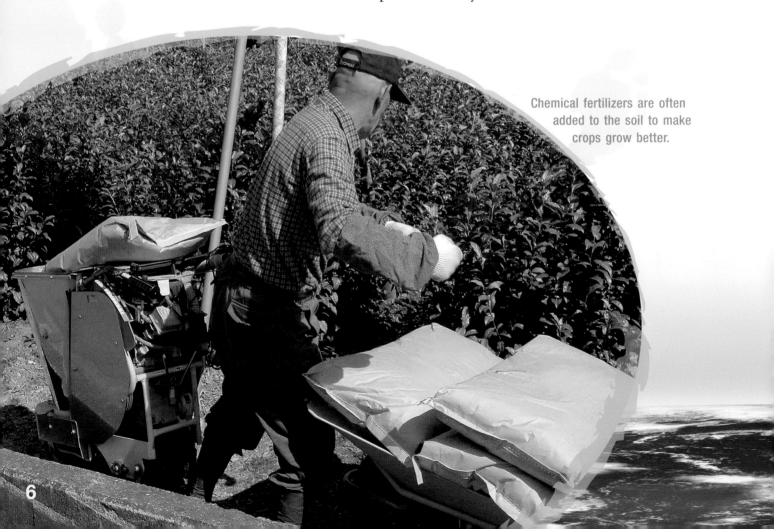

Chemical fertilizers are often added to the soil to make crops grow better.

Premium
Mixed Bell Peppers
6 Pack
Class I #60357
PLU#4688
PLU#4682
PLU#4689
PRODUCE OF ISRAEL
AGREXCO LTD
121 KAHASHMONAIM ST, TEL-AVIV 61206, ISRAEL
FAX: 972-3-5630918

These peppers grown in Israel are about to be transported to the United States.

Food Transportation

Aircraft and ships sometimes transport food that will be sold on the other side of the world. For local deliveries, refrigerated trucks keep food cool while it is being transported, so it stays fresh for longer.

Food Processing

Processed food is food that has been made ready to eat. Today, processed foods include everything from washed salads to granola bars to complete meals that only need to be heated up before being eaten.

Food Shopping

Shopping for food is now easier than ever before. Everything people need is gathered together in supermarkets. They have to visit only one store to buy meat, fish, fresh fruit and vegetables, and other goods.

Benefits of the Food Industry

Today's food industry has many benefits.

⊕ Food can be kept fresh for longer.

⊕ Food can be transported far away from where it is grown, so people in cold countries can eat food grown in warmer places.

⊕ For many people, food has become cheaper than ever before.

⊕ The food industry has been able to feed most of the world's population, which is four times as big today as it was one hundred years ago.

⊕ Supermarkets, fast food, and frozen or prepared meals have all made feeding yourself quicker than ever before.

Thanks to modern transportation, people can enjoy a varied diet throughout the year, such as fruit that cannot be grown locally in winter.

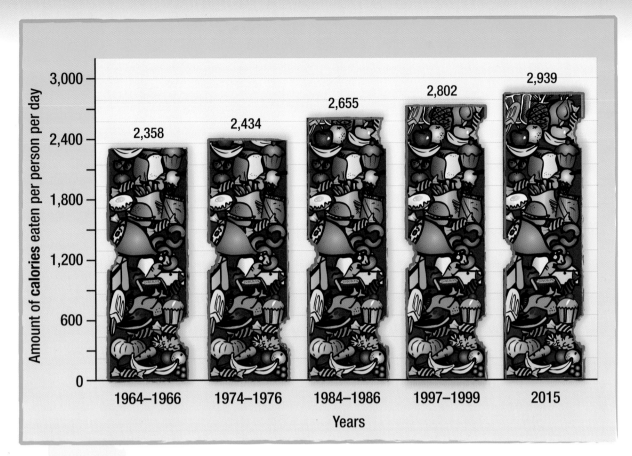

Today, people eat more food than ever before, making their footprints even heavier.

Costs of the Food Industry

Today's food industry has many costs to the environment.

- ⊕ The chemicals used to increase crop sizes can harm the soil and kill plants and animals in surrounding areas.
- ⊕ Irrigation of crops is leading to water shortages in many parts of the world.
- ⊕ Food processing uses energy, causes **pollution**, and creates waste.
- ⊕ Transporting food causes pollution.
- ⊕ Food packaging adds to a constantly growing mountain of waste.

All these things harm the environment and make food footprints heavier. If people keep making heavy footprints, in the future it may be difficult to grow enough food for everyone.

Farming

Modern farming methods can leave heavy footprints on the environment. It is, however, possible to buy food that has left only a light footprint behind.

Land Clearing for Farms

In areas such as the Amazon region of South America, undeveloped land is cleared to make space for farms. The people, animals, and plants that lived there lose their homes.

Many plants that can be used to make medicine have been discovered in the Amazon. There may be more undiscovered plants that could lead to more medical breakthroughs in the future. When the forest is cut down, these undiscovered plants may disappear forever.

Irrigation

Farming uses a lot of water. Some crops need more water than is provided by rain, so farmers add extra water. This is called irrigation. In places where not much rain falls, irrigation is slowly using up water stores and running rivers dry.

Rethink!

Eating less beef can reduce your food footprint. If there was less demand for beef, less land would be cleared to make space for cattle farms.

This area of the Amazon region, once covered in rain forest, has been cleared for cattle grazing.

Case Study
Farming in a Dry Land

The Murray–Darling Basin is the main river system in Australia, the world's second driest continent (after Antarctica). The basin supplies water to irrigate farms that produce over 40 percent of Australia's food. Rice, cotton, and other crops that require a lot of water are grown in the region.

Growing crops that need irrigation has two main effects:

⊕ Reserves of water are being used up. In December 2006, the basin was reported to be 54 percent below its previously recorded minimum. If the reserves are used up, it may become difficult to grow any crops.

⊕ The soil is being ruined. Adding water to the soil draws up salts that have been stored below the surface. Eventually, the soil becomes so salty that plants cannot grow in it.

Rice crops in the Murray–Darling Basin of Australia do not survive without irrigation.

Bees spread pollen from flowers, which helps the plants to reproduce. Pesticides harm these useful insects.

Pesticides

On many large farms, chemicals called pesticides are used. Pesticides stop pests, such as weeds, insects, and **fungi**, from spoiling the crops. But pesticides spread out, killing creatures in the surrounding area, where insects, weeds, and fungi are doing important jobs. The insects help plants to **reproduce**. The weeds provide food for animals. The fungi help turn dead plants into soil. Because pesticides harm the environment, food grown by using them has a heavy footprint.

Fertilizers and Soil

Fertilizers are used to grow bigger crops. They provide extra nutrients to the plants. Each time a farmer plants a crop, more chemical fertilizer must be added to the soil. This means that the soil slowly loses its natural nutrients, and it becomes harder to grow food in it without fertilizer.

Fertilizers and Water

When it rains, fertilizers can be washed off the soil and into streams and rivers. Here, they help some plants grow quickly. These fast-growing plants take over, making it impossible for other plants and animals to survive. Fertilizers from farms have damaged environments such as the Great Barrier Reef in Australia and the Kalamazoo River in the United States.

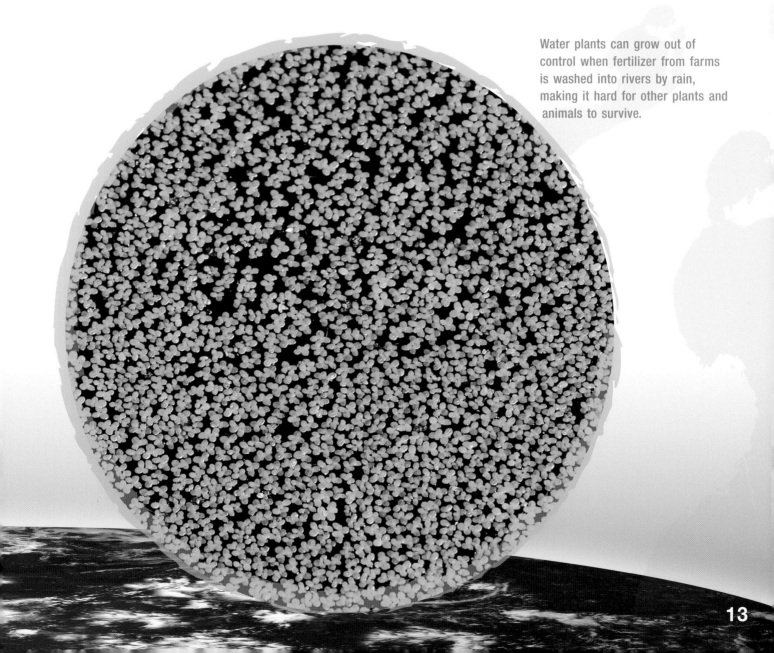

Water plants can grow out of control when fertilizer from farms is washed into rivers by rain, making it hard for other plants and animals to survive.

Organic farmers spread compost to help plants grow, instead of using chemical fertilizer.

Organic Farming

Organic farming is a way of growing food without using chemicals. Not using pesticides means that local plants and animals are not accidentally killed when the pesticides spread to other areas. Instead of fertilizers, organic farmers use compost, which makes the soil better for the plants and does not affect nearby rivers and streams.

Organic farmers often use crop rotation. This means that the same fields are used to grow different crops. The soil gets a rest, and is naturally able to recover the nutrients that were taken out of it by growing plants. This means that people in the future will still be able to grow food on that soil without using chemicals.

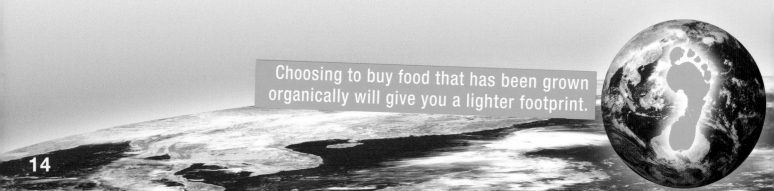

Choosing to buy food that has been grown organically will give you a lighter footprint.

An Organic Farm

Demand for organic food has led to increasing numbers of organic farms. One example is Sheepdrove organic farm in the United Kingdom.

Sheepdrove is a mixed organic farm. This means it produces a combination of meat, poultry, and plant crops.

The farm uses crop rotation. It grows grains, field beans, and some herbs. These take nutrients from the soil, so leys are also grown. Leys are cloverlike plants that help the soil to recover its goodness, and are also food for animals.

This system gives the soil time to recover before the same crops are planted in it again.

These turkeys enjoy roaming freely at Sheepdrove organic farm and help the farmer by eating insect pests.

Food Processing

Food processing includes sorting, cooking, and packaging food to make it ready for sale. Food processing uses energy and natural resources. Food that uses more of these has a heavier footprint.

Factory Food

Raw food is usually taken to factories once it has been harvested. There it is prepared for sale, or processed. Processing might involve cleaning vegetables and sorting them into plastic bags. Or it could be taking raw ingredients and cooking them before sealing them in cans or other containers. Then the food is transported to wherever it will be sold.

Rethink!

Lots of food packaging can be **recycled** instead of being thrown away.

Food packaged for sale creates a lot of extra waste.

Transporting Food

Transporting food to and from the processing factory adds extra distance to the journey it makes before being eaten. The vehicles that transport food cause pollution. The more "food miles" the food travels, the more damaging air pollution it causes.

Packaging Processed Food

Processed food needs to be packaged to make it **hygienic**, easy to transport, and appealing to customers. It often has more packaging than unprocessed food.

Wasted Food

Some big food growers throw away food that could be eaten. They do this because the food does not look as attractive, and customers might not buy it. Crooked carrots, pitted potatoes, and bananas without a bend may all be thrown away because they do not look right. This means that all the resources used to grow the food have been wasted.

Some stores avoid wasting less-than-perfect fruit and vegetables by selling them at a discount price.

Cooking Food

How food is cooked can have a big impact on the environment. This is because cooking food requires energy. Where the energy comes from affects the food's footprint on the environment.

Fossil Fuels

Fossil fuels are coal, gas, and oil. These fuels cannot be replaced once they have been used up. People use fossil fuels for cooking in several ways.

- Gas is used for cooking on stoves, on some grills, and in ovens.

- Coal and oil are burned to make electricity to power electric stoves and microwaves. Burning coal and oil causes air pollution, which harms Earth's **atmosphere**.

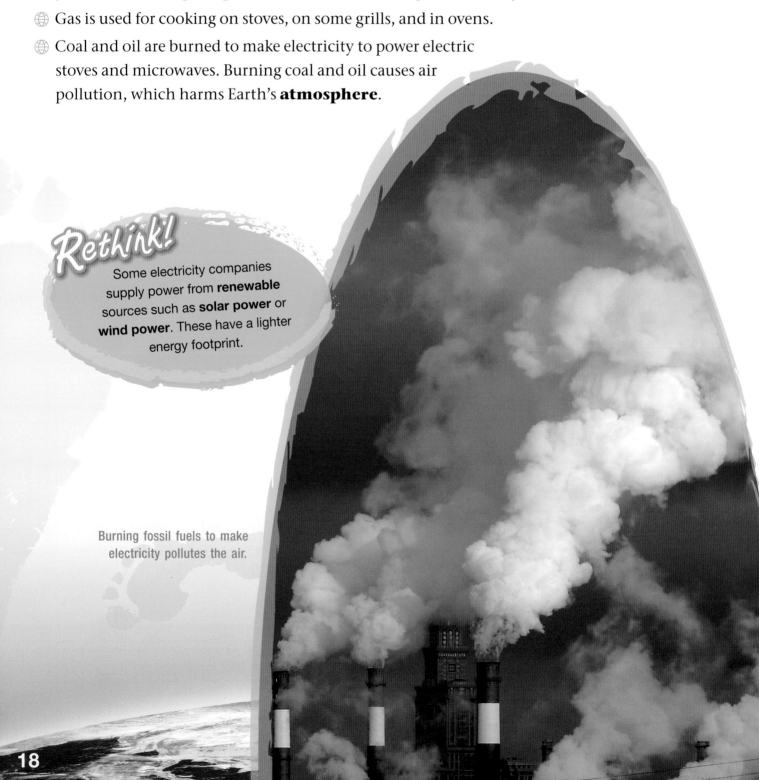

Rethink!

Some electricity companies supply power from **renewable** sources such as **solar power** or **wind power**. These have a lighter energy footprint.

Burning fossil fuels to make electricity pollutes the air.

Burning charcoal
to fuel a grill
produces pollution.

Wood and Charcoal

Around the world, many people burn wood or **charcoal** to cook food. This has two main effects on the environment.

- The smoke causes pollution.
- Forests that are cut down for wood or charcoal are sometimes not replanted. On hilly land, this causes the soil to be washed away by rain. This leaves a heavy footprint, because it means that no trees can grow there in the future.

Trees help the environment by taking in polluting **carbon dioxide** and releasing **oxygen**. Cutting trees down harms the environment, but planting new ones helps reduce the amount of carbon dioxide in the atmosphere.

Choosing to buy food that has been processed, cooked, and packaged in ways that are not wasteful and do not cause pollution will give you a lighter food footprint.

Food Transportation

Food is often transported a long way before it is eaten. Transporting food causes pollution, which harms the environment. If transporting food has caused a lot of pollution, the food has a heavy footprint.

Distance Traveled

The distance food travels is one of the things that affects its footprint. Food transportation is often expressed in "food miles." The farther food travels, the more food miles it has, and the more likely it is to have a heavy footprint.

Even a simple fruit salad like this one may have traveled thousands of miles before being eaten.

Rethink!

Most food is labeled to show where it comes from. Food that has been grown nearby has the lightest food footprint.

20

Types of Transportation

The way food is transported affects its footprint. This is because some types of transportation cause more pollution than others.

- Air travel is the biggest polluter. Airplanes release more carbon dioxide (a **greenhouse gas**) into the air than other forms of transportation. They also release the carbon dioxide high in the air, where it does more damage than it would nearer to the ground.

- Road transportation is another source of pollution. Trucks and cars release carbon dioxide, but not as much as airplanes do.

- Rail and water transportation are the least polluting ways to transport food. They have the lightest footprints.

Air transportation is by far the most polluting way to import and export food.

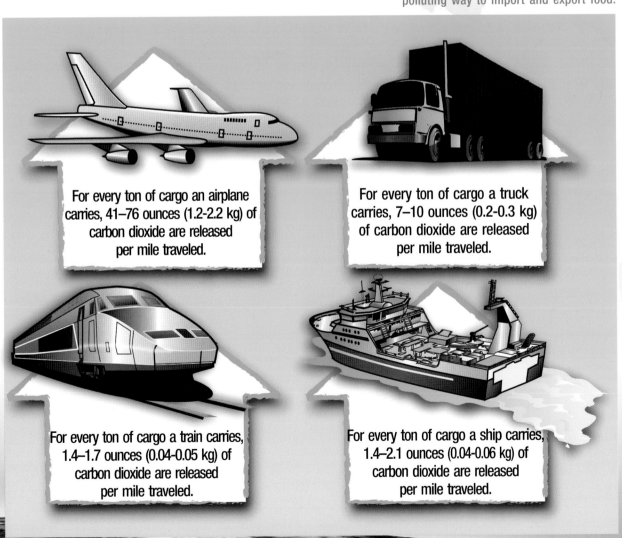

For every ton of cargo an airplane carries, 41–76 ounces (1.2-2.2 kg) of carbon dioxide are released per mile traveled.

For every ton of cargo a truck carries, 7–10 ounces (0.2-0.3 kg) of carbon dioxide are released per mile traveled.

For every ton of cargo a train carries, 1.4–1.7 ounces (0.04-0.05 kg) of carbon dioxide are released per mile traveled.

For every ton of cargo a ship carries, 1.4–2.1 ounces (0.04-0.06 kg) of carbon dioxide are released per mile traveled.

Seasonal Food

Seasonal food is food that only grows at certain times of year. For example, in northern California, berries such as strawberries and raspberries first ripen in May. If northern Californians want to eat strawberries in March, the fruit has to come from somewhere warmer. This means it has to be transported from the warmer place. This causes pollution, and makes the strawberries' footprint bigger.

In-season food is food that grows naturally in the current local season. Because in-season food grows nearby, the food does not have to be transported long distances. Eating food that is in season near where you live helps reduce your food footprint.

Eating locally grown fruit in season makes your food footprint lighter.

Choosing to buy food that is in season and grown and manufactured near your home will give you a lighter food footprint.

Case Study
Farmers' Markets

Farmers' markets are increasingly popular as a way of reducing food footprints. This is because local farmers bring their produce to the market for sale. The food does not travel long distances before being eaten, so it has a lighter footprint.

There are farmers' markets in towns and cities all around the world, from New York City, in the United States, to Sydney, in Australia.

A typical farmers' market takes place once a week. Many local farmers bring their produce to the market to sell. This includes eggs, fresh fruit and vegetables, cheese, meat, seafood, bread and cakes, and a large variety of other foods.

Local people can walk to a farmers' market instead of driving, which creates less pollution.

Food Packaging

A lot of food is sold packaged in paper, plastic, or metal. Food packaging uses up valuable natural resources. Food with a lot of packaging has a heavy environmental footprint.

Natural Resources

Most food packaging is made from natural resources such as:

- metal for cans
- oil to make plastic
- wood for paper and cardboard

Resources such as metal and oil will run out more quickly if people continue buying packaged food.

Rethink!

Some stores let customers bring their own containers to fill with foods such as rice or granola. This avoids new packaging altogether.

Iron ore from this mine is used to make metal cans for food packaging.

Garbage dumps are full of food packaging that will not decompose.

Energy

Food packaging is often made in big paper or plastics factories. These factories use up energy. The energy usually comes from burning fossil fuels, which pollutes the environment. If food has unnecessary packaging, this energy has been wasted, and the environment has been damaged. Extra packaging gives food a heavier footprint.

Waste

Food packaging thrown away as garbage creates waste. This harms the environment because some of the waste does not rot away and disappear. Instead, it hangs around for thousands of years. The piles of waste are getting bigger and bigger, yet every year people create more waste.

Avoiding Packaging

People who want a smaller food footprint have begun to find ways to avoid buying packaged foods. They try to choose food that comes without packaging, such as bananas in a bunch instead of a plastic bag. Bananas have their own wrapper, after all!

Recycling

Recycling food packaging helps lighten its environmental footprint. The materials in food packaging can be made into useful products. For example, old plastic bottles can be recycled to make clothes. Most food packaging is labeled to show whether or not it can be recycled. Recycling, however, uses energy. This means that recyclable packaging still has a heavier footprint than no packaging at all.

Product of Australia
Bananas

9 300601 186150

BEST BEFORE: 27.10.07
V.C 944210

AUSTRALIAN CERTIFIED ORGANIC

Organic

Rethink!

Disposable plastic bags waste resources. Say "no" to plastic and carry your shopping in a reusable cloth bag instead.

Avoiding unnecessary packaging and choosing to buy food in recyclable packaging or packaging that will decompose will give you a lighter food footprint.

Clothes from Plastic Drink Bottles

Recycled plastic from beverage bottles can be used to make fleecy cloth. Old plastic bottles are chopped into flakes to be cleaned, then blown dry to get rid of any dust. The flakes are melted and then squeezed through tiny holes. This turns them into tiny threads. These threads are then woven into a cloth called post-consumer recycled fleece or PCR fleece.

It takes just twenty-five 2-liter soft drink bottles to make a fleece jacket that fits an adult.

The fabric in this fleece jacket is made from recycled drink bottles.

How Big Is Your Food Footprint?

The size of people's food footprints depends on how their food is grown, transported, packaged, and even how it is cooked. How big do you think your footprint is?

How Is Your Food Grown?

Food with a light environmental footprint has been grown:

⊕ without chemicals that harm the soil or local environment

⊕ without using more water than is naturally available

⊕ on land that has been farmland for a long time, rather than land that has been cleared of native vegetation to become farmland in the last few years

How Was Your Food Transported?

Food grown outside your front door would have the lightest transportation footprint. Carrying it into the kitchen would not cause pollution! The food that does least harm to the environment has:

⊕ not traveled very far

⊕ been transported using the least polluting method possible

How big do you think your food footprint is?

Food labeling carries information that can help people figure out its environmental footprint.

How Is Your Food Packaged?

The more packaging a food comes in, the worse it is for the environment. If food does have to be packaged, the best packaging is the kind that can be recycled or reused, such as a cloth bag. Packaging that is simply thrown away is a waste.

How Is Your Food Cooked?

Food that is cooked using lots of energy is bad for the environment, because making the energy causes pollution. Cooking different foods together saves energy and makes the food's environmental footprint lighter.

Recycling plastic, paper, and metal packaging is a good way to lighten your footprint.

Thinking about how food is grown, transported, packaged, and cooked will help you choose food with a lighter environmental footprint.

Future Food Footprints

You can choose to take light footsteps or heavy footsteps. If people continue leaving heavy footprints, it could affect the environment for thousands of years to come.

What You Can Do

The Internet is a great way to find out more about what you can do to take lighter footsteps. Try visiting these websites:

⊕ **http://www.ams.usda.gov/farmersmarkets**
This site has information about farmers' markets across the United States.

⊕ **http://www.nature.org/initiatives/climatechange/calculator/**
This site allows you to calculate the size of your carbon footprint. It includes questions about home energy, travel, food and diet, and recycling and waste.

⊕ **http://www.wwoofinternational.org/**
Find out about volunteering as a "Willing Worker On an Organic Farm." Volunteers work unpaid on organic farms throughout the world. In return, they get to enjoy country living and learn about organic farming.

Some of the search terms you might use to find interesting information about food and the environment include:

⊕ food packaging
⊕ preservatives
⊕ crop irrigation
⊕ organic farming.

In the future, one challenge will be feeding the world's people without harming the environment.

What will YOU do to change your food footprint in the future?

Glossary

atmosphere
the layer of gases that surrounds Earth, enabling humans, animals, and plants to survive

calories
units of measure for the energy in food

carbon dioxide
a gas that is used by plants to help them grow, and which is released when fossil fuels are burned

charcoal
a fuel made from partly burned wood

environment
the natural world, including plants, animals, land, rivers, and seas

farmers' markets
markets where farmers bring their crops to sell directly to the public

fertilizers
materials that help crops to grow; some fertilizers are natural, while others are artificially made using chemicals

fossil fuels
the remains of plants and animals from millions of years ago, which have been buried deep under Earth's surface and there turned into coal, oil, and gas

fungi
plantlike organisms that have no leaves or flowers, which often live off rotting plants

greenhouse gas
gas that contributes to global warming, which is often released when fossil fuels are burned

harvest
pick when fully grown or ready to eat

hygienic
clean and safe

irrigation
supplying water to a dry area to help crops grow

natural resources
natural substances, such as wood, metal, coal, or water, which can be used by humans

organic farming
growing produce without the use of artificial fertilizers or pesticides

oxygen
common gas that has no color or smell, which humans breathe and fires use to burn

packaging
the cardboard boxes, plastic bags, cans, or foam cartons that are used to wrap up food so it is ready for people to buy

pesticides
poisonous chemicals used to kill pests, such as insects, fungi, and weeds, to prevent them from damaging crops

pollution
damaging substances, such as chemicals or waste products, that harm the environment

processing
changing or preparing in a special way

recycled
used material from an old, worn-out product to make a new product

renewable
capable of being easily replaced

reproduce
make again

solar power
power from the Sun, which can be turned into electricity by solar panels

wind power
power that comes from the wind, which can be turned into electricity by windmills and wind turbines

Index

A

air transportation, 21
Amazon, 10

C

calories, 9
carbon dioxide, 19, 21
cattle grazing, 10
charcoal (as fuel), 19
chemicals, 6, 9, 14, 28
compost, 14
cooking, 16, 18–19, 29
crop rotation, 14, 15

E

environmental footprints, 4

F

farmers' markets, 23, 30
farming, 6, 9, 10–15, 28
fertilizers, 6, 9, 13, 14
food footprint, 5, 28–29
food industry, 6–9
fossil fuels, 18, 24

G

greenhouse gases, 17, 18, 19, 21

I

insects, 12
irrigation, 6, 9, 10, 30

L

land clearing, 10, 19

M

Murray–Darling Basin, 11

N

natural resources, 4, 25

O

organic farming, 14, 15, 30

P

packaging, 9, 16, 17, 24–27, 29, 30
pesticides, 6, 12, 14
plastic bags, 26
pollution, 9, 13, 17, 18, 19, 20, 21
population growth, 4, 8
post-consumer recycled fleece, 27
processing food, 7, 16–19

R

rail transportation, 21
recycling, 16, 26, 27
refrigeration, 7
renewable power sources, 18
rice, 11
road transportation, 21

S

salt, 11, 12–13, 14
seasonal food, 22
shipping, 21
shopping, 7, 8, 23, 24
supermarkets, 7, 8

T

transportation, 7, 8, 9, 17, 20–21, 22, 28

W

waste, 9, 17, 25
water shortages, 10, 11
wood (as fuel), 19